DOMINIE READERS

The Other Side of the World

Story by Janie Spaht Gill, Ph.D.
Illustrations by Bob Reese

DOMINIE PRESS
Pearson Learning Group

Sitting on a bench,
Gary read an ad one day.

"Travel the world, visit fun
New Orleans...
best town in the whole U.S.A."

TRAVEL THE WORLD

VISIT FUN

NEW ORLEANS

Best tour in the whole USA

"New Orleans must be on the world's other side; to get there I must dig down."

4

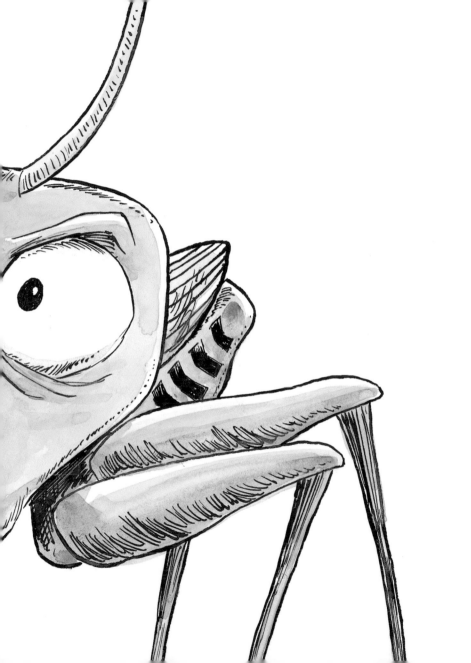

So Gary Grasshopper
started digging
a deep tunnel
down into the ground.

Passing an ant in the tunnel,
he stopped the red ant to say,

"I'm off to the world's
other side."

"Go west," said the ant.
"It's hilly,
and it's a very long way."

Digging west in the hilly
tunnel, he stopped by
a spider to say,
  "I'm off to
      the world's other side."

          "Go east," said
          the spider. "It's rocky,
          but it's not far away."

UP!

12

Digging east in the rocky tunnel, he stopped by an earthworm to say, "I'm off to the world's other side."

"Go up," said the earthworm. "You'll get there today."

13

Pulling himself from the tunnel,
Gary took a long look around.

Masked people on floats
were throwing some beads;
bands played a loud
marching sound.

17

"I've arrived," Gary said,
"on the world's other side.

The best town
in the whole U.S.A."

Gary never found out he had traveled just three feet and peeked out of his tunnel on Mardi Gras Day!

21

The Other Side of the World

■ Direct the children's attention to the fact that *grasshopper* and *earthworm* are made up of two words that are combined as one. Have them name other compound words: *ladybug*, *butterfly*, etc. Write the compound words on a sentence strip and have the children divide each compound word into its two components.

■ Have the children make Mardi Gras masks out of tag board, with holes cut out for the eyes. The masks can be decorated with scrap materials (glitter, sequins, stars, crepe paper, ribbons, beads, etc.) and colored with colored markers. The children can then glue the masks onto rulers or small sticks and hoist them into the air.

■ Use this opportunity to locate New Orleans on a map of the United States. Discuss the fact that the Mardi Gras holiday is a day of parades, floats, and costumes. Have the children name other parades they have seen and other occasions on which they have worn costumes. Write the months of the year on the board with the parades next to the month in which they occurred.

■ Help the children develop oral language by naming other animals that live under the ground. After you write these animal names on the board, have the children draw one of them on a sheet of paper.

About the Author

Dr. Janie Spaht Gill brings twenty-five years of teaching experience to her books for young children. During her career thus far, she has taught at every grade level, from kindergarten through college. Gill has a Ph.D. in reading education, with a minor in creative writing. She is currently residing in Lafayette, Louisiana with her husband, Richard. Her fresh, humorous topics are inspired by the things her students say in the classroom. Gill was voted the 1999-2000 Louisiana Elementary Teacher of the Year for her outstanding work in primary education.

Softcover Edition ISBN 0-7685-2165-3
Library Bound Edition ISBN 0-7685-2473-3

Printed in Singapore
          12 13 14 V0ZF 14 13 12 11

Dominie Press
Pearson Learning Group

1-800-321-3106
www.pearsonlearning.com